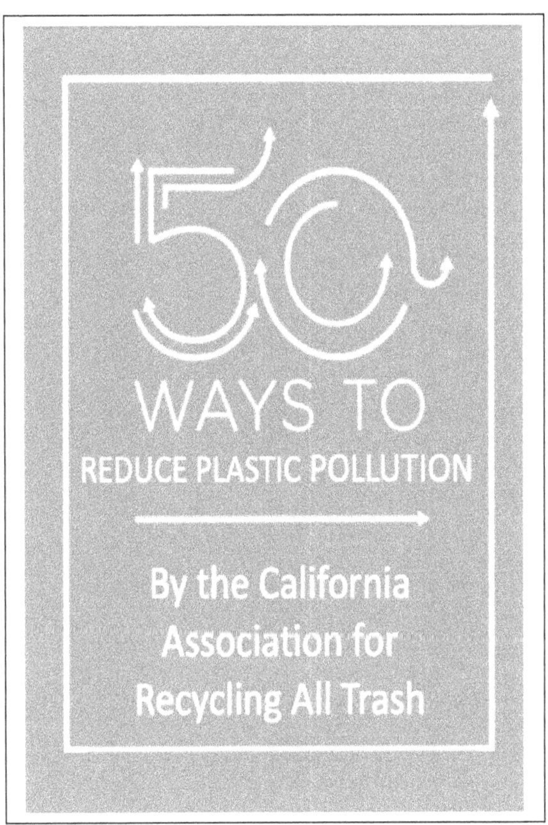
50
WAYS TO
REDUCE PLASTIC POLLUTION

By the California
Association for
Recycling All Trash

**California Assocation for
Recycling All Trash (CARAT)**

**Inprint Books
La Jolla, California**

Table of Contents

Introduction

In the postwar years there was a shift in American perceptions as plastics were no longer seen as entirely positive. Plastic debris in the oceans was first observed in the 1960s, a decade in which Americans became increasingly aware of environmental problems. Rachel Carson's 1962 book, *Silent Spring*, exposed the dangers of chemical pesticides. In 1969 a major oil spill occurred off the Santa Barbara, California coast and the polluted Cuyahoga River in Ohio caught fire, raising concerns about pollution. As awareness about environmental issues spread, the persistence of plastic waste began to trouble Americans.

Plastic also gradually became a word used to describe that which was cheap, flimsy, or fake. In *The Graduate*, one of the top movies of 1967, Dustin Hoffman's character was urged by an older acquainttance to make a career in plastics. Audiences cringed along with Hoffman at what they saw as misplaced enthusiasm for an industry that, rather than being full of possibilities, was a symbol of cheap conformity and superficiality.

Plastic Problems: Waste and Health

Plastic's reputation fell further in the 1970s and 1980s as anxiety about waste increased. Plastic became a special target because, while so many plastic products are disposable, plastic lasts forever in the environment. It was the plastics industry that offered recycling as a solution. In the 1980s the plastics industry led an influential drive encouraging municipalities to collect and process recyclable materials as part of their waste-management systems. However, recycling is far from perfect, and most plastics still end up in landfills or in the environment. Grocerystore plastic bags have become a target for activists looking to ban one-use, disposable plastics, and several American cities have already passed bag bans. The ultimate symbol of the problem of plastic waste is the Great Pacific Garbage Patch, which has often been described as a swirl of plastic garbage the size of Texas floating in the Pacific Ocean.[1]

The reputation of plastics has suffered further because of a growing concern about the potential threat they pose to human health. These concerns focus on the additives (such as the much-discussed bisphenol A [BPA] and a class of chemicals called phthalates) that go into plastics during the manufacturing process, making them more flexible, durable and transparent. Some scientists and members of the public are concerned about evidence that these chemicals leach out of plastics and into our food, water and bodies. In very high doses these chemicals can disrupt the endocrine (or hormonal) system. Researchers worry particularly about the effects of these chemicals on children and what continued accumulation means for future generations.

There are at least ten times more plastic polluting the Atlantic Ocean than previously believed a new study has found.[2] The National Oceanography Center (NOC) study, the first to measure the "invisible" microplastics beneath the surface of the entire Atlantic Ocean, found that there were between 12-21 million metric tons (approximately 13-23 million U.S. tons) of them floating in the top 200 meters (approximately 656 feet under the surface. According to the National Oceanic and Atmospheric Administration, it takes a plastic bottle 450 years to biodegrade.

---

[1] National Geographic Society.
[2] National Oceanographic Center, Southampton, England.

The Future of Plastics

Despite growing understanding of their environmental harm, plastics are critical to modern life. Plastics made possible the development of computers, cell phones, and most of the lifesaving advances of modern medicine. Lightweight and good for insulation, plastics help save fossil fuels used in heating and in transportation. Perhaps most importantly, inexpensive plastics raised the standard of living and made material abundance more readily available. With-out plastics many possessions that we take for granted might be out of reach for all but the richest citizens. Replacing natural materials with plastic has made many of our possessions cheaper, lighter, safer and stronger.

Since it's clear that plastics have a valuable place in our lives, some scientists are attempting to make plas-tics safer and more sustainable. Some innovators are developing bioplastics, which are made from plants instead of fossil fuels, to create substances that are more environmentally friendly than convention-al plastics. Others are working to make plastics that are truly biodegradable. Some innovators are searching for ways to make recycling more efficient, and they even hope to perfect a process that converts plastics back into the fossil fuels from which they were derived. All of these innovators recognize that plastics are not perfect but that they are an important and necessary part of our future.

Some key facts:

- Half of all plastics ever manufactured have been made
  in the last 15 years.[3]
- Production of plastics has increased exponentially,
  from 2.3 million tons in 1950 to 448 million tons by
  2015. Production is expected to double by 2050.[4]
- Every year, about eight million tons of plastic waste
  escapes into the oceans from coastal nations. That's
  the equivalent of setting five garbage bags full of trash
  on every foot of coastline around the world.[5]
- Plastics often contain additives making them stronger,
  more flexible, and durable. But many of these
  additives can extend the life of products if they
  become litter, with some estimates ranging to at least
  400 years to break down.[6]
- What happens when a marine animal eats a piece of
  plastic? The plastic can end up, undigested, in the
  animal's belly. This was the case when scientists
  discovered a dead sperm whale (*Physeter
  macrocephalus*) with 22 kilograms (50 pounds) of
  plastic of all sizes—from drinking cups to flip-flops—
  in its stomach. Ingested trash like this can hurt and
  clog the digestive tract, leaving little room for real
  food. This can be observed in a great variety of
  animals, with seabirds particularly affected.[7]

---

[3] *The Atlantic,* July 19, 2017.

[4] *University of Rhode Island Magazine,* Fall, 2020. *"World's
Plastic Pollution Crisis Explained."*

[5] *National Geographic,* June 7, 2019. [6] *National Geographic,*
June 7, 2019.

[7] *USA Today,* April 1, 2019.

- The average person eats at least 50,000 particles of
  microplastic a year and breathes in a similar quantity,

according to the first study to estimate human ingestion of plastic pollution. The true number of plastic particles eaten by the average person is likely to be many times higher, as only a small number of foods and drinks have been analysed for plastic contamination. Scientists have reported that drinking a lot of water from plastic bottles drastically increased the particles consumed.[8]

- The health impacts of ingesting microplastic are unknown, but they could release toxic substances. Some pieces are small enough to penetrate human tissues, where they could trigger immune reactions.

- Microplastic pollution is mostly created by the disintegration of plastic litter and appears to be ubiquitous across the planet. Researchers have found microplastic particles everywhere they look—in the air, soil, rivers and the deepest oceans around the world.
- Plastics have been detected in tap and bottled water, seafood and beer. They were also found in human stool samples confirming that people ingest the particlcs.[9]
- Recent studies have shown that every person has thousands of microplastic particles in their brains, heart and arteries and that After nearly three years, the rate of heart attack, stroke and death was 4.5 times higher in people with microplastics in their plaque than those without.[10]

---

8. *The Guardian,* June 5, 2019.
9. *Time* magazine, May 29, 2019.
- 10 New England Journal of Medicine, March 7, 2024.

microplastic particles in fish, shellfish, sugar, salt, beer and water, as well as in the air in cities. The scientists then used U.S. government dietary to Adults eat about 50,000 microplastic particles a year and children about 40,000, they estimated.[11]

- Scientists have described a new disease called plasticosis, caused by ingesting microplastic particles, in seabirds. Scientists have described a new disease called plasticosis, which is directly caused by plastic waste in the environment.[11] While the disease has so far only been identified in the digestive tracts of seabirds, the scale of the problem suggests it could be widespread in other species and different parts of the body. For the new study, scientists from London's Natural History Museum have now examined the ill effects on the health of a seabird species known as flesh-footed shearwaters, which previous studies have found to be among the most plastic-contaminated birds in the world. In doing so, the team found that the birds' symptoms were so consistent that it warranted describing a new disease. Plasticosis got its name due to its similarity to other fibrotic diseases caused by inorganic materials, like silicosis and asbestosis. Tiny shards of plastic become lodged in the birds' digestive tracts, causing chronic inflammation and scarring that leads to a host of other problems. The team found that exposure to microplastics inflames microplastics inflames and scars the proventriculus, the first chamber of their stomach, until it eventually starts to break down.

11. *The Guardian,* March 3, 2023.

That can stunt the glands that secrete digestive compounds, which can affect their vitamin absorption and make them more vulnerable to infection and parasites. In extreme cases, chicks can starve to death because their stomachs become full of undigestible plastic.

For those that survive, plasticosis seems to stunt their growth. Larger amounts of plastic were associated with smaller overall weight and shorter wings.

So far, plasticosis has only been documented in the digestive systems of these flesh-footed shearwaters, but given how common the pollutant is, the team says it's likely that the disease affects other species as well and could cause similar scarring in other parts of the body. Investigating this could be an important step for future work. The research was published in the *Journal of Hazardous Materials*.

- Plastics are entering the food chain through plants.[12] This work provided insights into the uptake pro-cess of polystyrene microplastics in strawberry plants using confocal laser scanning microscopy and scanning electron microscopy. "Our results clearly showed that PS-MPs can enter the root of strawberry and be trans-ported to the shoot via the apoplastic pathway. The critical sites for introducing polystyrene

---

12. *Journal of Hazardous Materials*, Volume 449, May 5, 2023.

microplastics into roots were shown to be the apical zone and lateral root emergence sites." Considering

the large quantity of global plastics waste, concerns about microplastics pollution in terrestrial ecosystems are growing. Microplastics can penetrate plant roots, move upward to the aboveground portions, and finally enter the food chain.

In summary, plastic pollution is everywhere. Humans throw it into rivers, landfills, lakes, streams and the ocean where it has accumulated in massive amounts. Plastic pollution threatens fish, wildlife, bees and humans.

We need to take drastic action to regulate the use and disposal of all products and packaging that use plastics. We can no longer be guinea pigs.

Part I

Grocery Shopping

1. Use Biodegradable, Compostable Plastic Bags

Each year approximately 500 billion to one trillion plastic bags are used worldwide.[13]

Most plastics are made from petroleum. However, functionally similar materials can be made from polylactic acid (PLA), which is typically made from plant starch. The other main type of bioplastic is made from polyhydroxyalkanoates (PHAs). PHAs are longchain polyesters produced by microorganisms and plants. Both types of material are called bioplastics. You will also see them referred to as biodegradable plastics and compostable plastics. Despite the name, not all bioplastic products biodegrade naturally or break down in a compost bin.

One product category where biodegradability makes the most sense is plastic bags. Even when they are made of a recyclable polymer, plastic bags can't go in the regular recycling in most communities. A few curbside programs accept plastic bags, but more

---

[13] "Store offers biodegradable bags." Aiken Standard (Aiken, South Carolina (February 17, 2009).

often, they must be delivered to special collection bins– which are not available everywhere.

Biodegradable Plastic Bags

Trader Joe's, a national grocery chain in the United States, uses Crown Poly biodegradable plastic bags. The Crown Poly Compostable Bags are made from 100% vegetable starches which make them fully biodegradable and compostable. These bags are certified for both commercial and home composting and will biodegrade within 180 days. Trader Joe's uses these bags without being forced to buy a government agency. But a government agency should compel stores to use biodegradable bags and ban the use of regular plastic bags. Trader Joe's would not voluntarily use biodegradable plastic bags if they were significantly more expensive than ordinary plastic bags.

Bioplastics, or specifically bioplastic resins, are understood as plastic resins that are combined from starch (wheat starch, corn, potatoes, etc.) and ordinary plastic resins (derived from petroleum) that have been broken. polymer bonding. Depending on the type of product produced, the mixing ratio between coffee grounds and ordinary plastic granules is regulated, up to a maximum of 50% starch. The most commonly used bioplastic is PLA, polylactic acid.

- Bioplastic, also known as organic plastic, is defined as a plastic derived from living organisms and formed from renewable materials from nature such as corn flour, rice flour, potatoes, cassava ... or by variable microorganisms that have the potential to have a positive impact on the environment. Biodegradable bioplastics are plastics that, under the influence of microorganisms, will be completely transformed into CO2, H20, biomass... Common types of biodegradable bioplastics are:

- PLA (polylactic acid) is a biological raw material for the production of plant starches such as corn, potatoes, cassava, etc.

- PHAs (polyhydroxyalkanoates)–these plastics can be made from microbial origin, applied in some cases in the medical field.

- Coffee Bio-composite: Bioplastic derived from 60% natural coffee.

The popularity of PLA bioplastics is much higher than that of PHAs, typically due to the application and field of application of the two different types.

Great features of PLA plastic:

PLA plastic looks and acts like polyethylene terephthalate (PET) and polypropylene, so it is difficult to distinguish PLA from traditional plastic by the eye.

Degradability: The decomposition time of PLA plastic is quite short, only a few months or a few years.

When affected by microorganisms, this bioplastic will completely decompose into carbon dioxide (CO_2) and water (H_2O), beneficial humus for the soil. This is the main factor that has created a lot of positive effects on the environment.

Environmental Benefits

According to NatureWorks, a company specializing in the production of bioplastics in the U.S., producing PLA bioplastics will save two-thirds of the energy compared to producing conventional plastics.

Unlike traditional plastic, when decomposed, PLA bioplastic does not increase the amount of CO^2 in the air very much. In particular, if buried (composted), when decomposed, they will produce 70% fewer greenhouse gases.

Whole Foods and other companies sell biodegradable plastic bags. **NaturBag** is shown on the next page.

You can buy NaturBags at www.naturebag.com.

Pooch Paper is a paper alternative to plastic dog waste bags. The product aims to solve a common problem for dog owners while being environmentally conscious. Pooch Paper is made from recycled paper and are both compostable and biodegradable. They offer a strong, leak-proof alternative to plastic bags for picking up dog waste. www.poochpaper.com.

2. Buy Products in Glass Jars and Cans or Without any Packaging

You can still find some products in glass jars and metal cans. Jelly, marmalade, pickles, pickled beets and many other food products are available in glass jars.

Buy fresh produce that is not wrapped in plastic. Glass jars make great containers for leftovers. Glass is also not a pollutant like plastic is.

3. Use Paper Bags for Produce (Mushrooms Keep Better in Paper Bags)

When I go to Whole Foods, I always use their paper bags to fill with produce, especially mushrooms. Mushrooms and most other produce, keeps better in paper bags than plastic. Avocados ripen better in paper bags.

4. Buy Powdered Laundry Detergent or Detergent Sheets

Over 700,000,000 single-use plastic laundry detergent jugs end up in landfills and oceans each year in the United States. Arm and Hammer, Hey Sunday, Earth Breeze, Clean People, Tru Earth,Sheets Laundry, Good Juju, Kind Laundry, Eco Roots, WashEZ and GroveCo make laundry sheets. Kind and Earth Breeze, Hey Sunday, Arm and Hammer are made in China. You can also purchase Tide powder in a cardboard box from Target and other retailers. Tide has just introduced Tide Evo, concentrated dissolvable tablets in cardboard packaging.

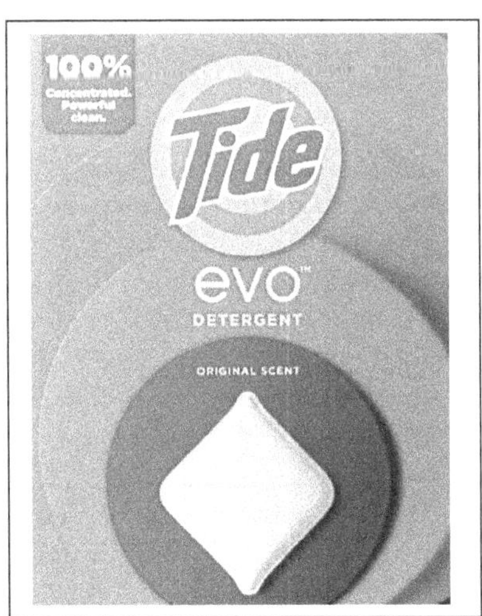

5. Don't Buy Filtered Cigarettes

You shouldn't smoke cigarettes for health reasons. The tobacco industry produces[14] an estimated six trillion filtered cigarettes a year,[15] making them a top contributor to a global plastic crisis. The tobacco industry's cigarette filters fraud could put us all in danger. The industry makes filters from microplastic fibers, which filter practically nothing.[16] Microplastics contaminate our soil, food, and water, and new studies suggest links to mutations in DNA.[17, 18] They're destroying our environment–and may wind up inside you and the ones you love.

[14] Zafeiridou M, Hopkinson NS, Voulvoulis N. Cigarette Smoking: An Assessment of Tobacco's Global Environmental Footprint Across Its Entire Supply Chain. Environmental Science & Technology. 2018.

[15] Novotny TE, Slaughter E. Tobacco Product Waste: An Environmental Approach to Reduce Tobacco Consumption. Curr Environ Health Rep. 2014;1(3):208-216.

[16] Proctor RN. Golden Holocaust: Origins of the Cigarette Catastrophe and the Case for Abolition. Berkeley, CA: University of California Press. 2011.

[17] Oliveri Conti G, Ferrante M, Banni M, et   al. "Micro-andnanoplastics in edible fruit and vegetables. The first diet risksassessment for the general population.Environ Res. 2020.

[18] Poma A, Vecchiotti G, Colafarina S, et al. In Vitro Genotoxicity of Polystyrene Nanoparticles on the Human Fibroblast Hs27 Cell Line. Nanomaterials (Basel) 2019.

Cigarette filters are made with plastic.

6. Use Natural Dental Floss

Eco-friendly floss is made of biodegradable silk thread spun and coated with natural beeswax or a plantderived wax. RADIUS®' silk is made with pure, inviting, luxurious silk and is free from the toxins found in similar products. It glides easily between teeth for a meticulously clean finish.

You can purchase silk floss and other alternatives at www.madebyradius.com; TreeBird Pure Silk Eco Floss at Amazon; Wowe Biodegradable Silk Dental Floss at Amazon; Thrive Market Gentle Tape Dental Floss at Thrive Market; Dental Lace Zero Waste Refillable Silk Floss at Amazon; Georganics Dental Floss at Georganics.com; Best Disposable Packaging:

 The Humble Co. Interdental Brush Bamboo at Thehumble.co; Happy Eco Plant Based Floss Picks at Amazon.

NATURAL
FLOSS

**NO
PFAS**

PURE SILK
UNSCENTED

7. Don't Buy Plastic Forks, Spoons and Knives (Unless They are Plant-Based)

Plastic forks. Knives and spoons are wasteful one-use throwaways. It is better to use metal utenils and to wash them. If you must have disposal silverware, get plant-based biodegradable ones. You can buy them online at ecoproductsstore.com and forksoverknives.com.www.bamboodlers.com. Bamboo utensils are available at

8. Don't Buy Plastic Straws or Stirrers. Use Wood Stirrers

Plastic straws, plastic stirrers and plastic Q-tips are unnessary uses of plastic. The United States uses millions of single-use plastic straws a day.
Plastic straws are among the top 10 contributors to plastic marine debris across the globe.
Nearly 7.5 million plastic straws were found on U.S. shorelines during a five-year cleanup research project. Extrapolated globally, that is 437 million to 8.3 billion plastic straws on the world's coastlines.
Currently, plastic straws make up about 99% of the $3 billion global drinking-straw market.
Most recycling machines aren't capable of recycling straws, given their size.

As of November 1, 2021, New York City food service establishments may no longer provide single-use plastic beverage straws, except upon request.[19] Additionally, food service establishments may no longer provide single-use beverage splash sticks or stirrers made of plastic.

Options to Plastic Straws

- Beverage straws that are compostable and not made of plastic (for example. compostable paper)
- Beverage splash sticks and stirrers that are compostable and not made of plastic (for example, wood)

After a local 2nd grade student successfully petitioned the Portland City Council in 2018 to mitigate plastic straw use in city-owned buildings, the Maine Chapter took it to the next level with Council interest to pass a citywide ordinance becoming the first municipality in Maine to ban single-use plastic straws, stirrers and splash sticks![20]

The days of getting a plastic straw automatically with any drink are over in New Jersey.[21] In a bid to cut down on plastic pollution in the state, all coffee shops, restaurants, convenience stores and any other

------

[19] New York City Executive Order No. 54 February 6, 2020. [20] www.newscentermaine.com/article/news/local/portland/ portland-city-council-votes-to-ban-plastic-straws/97- 820a9186d72b-4aa0-91a2-fdbdfd5607fc.
[21] www.dailyprincetonian.com/article/2021/11/plastic- strawsban-new-jersey.

business that sells food can only give out plastic straws to customers who request them.

9. Buy a Metal Water Bottle

Studies have shown that plastic leaches from plastic water bottles into the water and thus into your body. Stainless steel water bottles are healthier for you and for the environment.

You will also save money by refilling your metal water bottle.

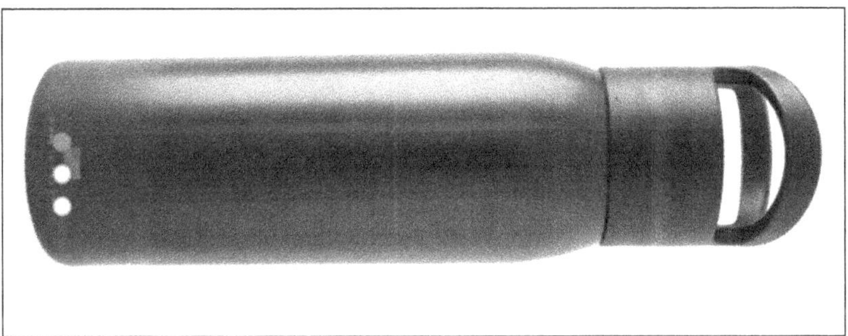

Liberty Bottle pictured above. Www.libertybottles.com.

10. Buy Natural Fiber Shopping Bags

Plastic shopping bags are wasteful. Shopping bags made out ofharmful to the environment. cotton canvas are durable and not

Part II
Clothing

11. Don't Buy Polyester Clothing-Buy Natural Fibers Like Cotton and Wool

Polyester tee shirts stink. According to Rachel McQueen, a textile scientist at the University of Alberta, polyester is hydrophobic, or water-hating. That means it's really great at soaking up sweat and then quickly getting rid of it through evaporation. This is what companies mean when they say a garment can "wick sweat," and it's what makes dry-fit workout tops so magical.

The problem is, polyester is oleophilic, a.k.a. oilloving. So while it wicks away plenty of watery eccrine sweat to keep you feeling dry, any of the oily apocrine sweat compounds and alreadydigested odorous compounds that pass through the clothing cling to polyester fibers for dear life.

There, they take on a new, especially foul kind of scent.

"Body odor itself is different on polyester," says McQueen. "People know it when they smell it. It's not your body odor, it's your body odor *on polyester.* It's a repulsive smell. And the reason for it is likely because of the selective way polyester will retain certain types of odorants." The kinds of odorous compounds that love to hang on to polyester combine to become especially pungent.

In addition, polyester is plastic. And does not biodegrade. You may sweat in cotton, but you won't smell as bad and you will feel good by doing your part for the environment.

12. Buy Leather or Cotton Belts not Plastic

Leather is a natural material. Of course, it comes from cows, but we eat cows don't we? To be a good vegan, you can buy or make a cotton or fiber-based belt. The cotton belt pictured below is from **Beltology** and it is made in New York City. Buy one at www.beltology.com.

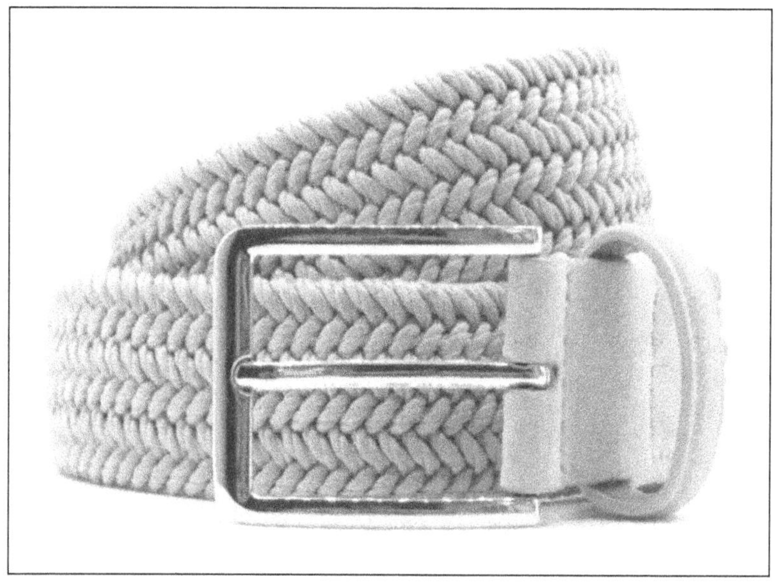

13. Buy Buttons Made of Natural Materials- Wood, Shells, Metal or Glass

Most buttons these days are made out of plastic. Keep on the lookout for shirts and coats made with buttons made out of natural materials. Some of my old polo shirts are made with Buffalo metal buttons. They are very durable. Metal buttons are shown below:

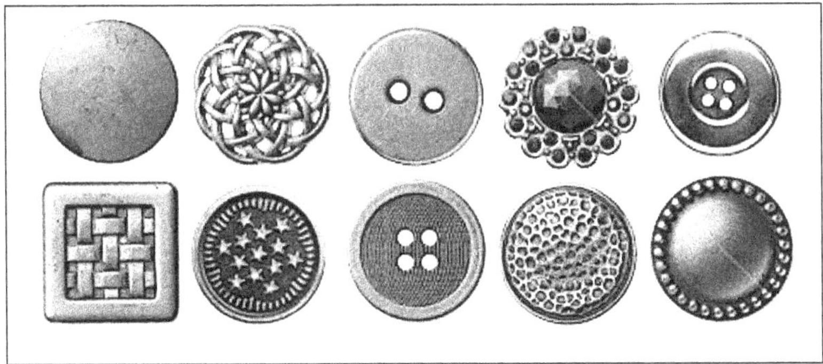

14. Buy Metal Zippers

Metal zippers are more reliable than plastic zippers. They grip better. They last longer. And they are not made out of nasty plastic. YKK metal zippers are pictured below:

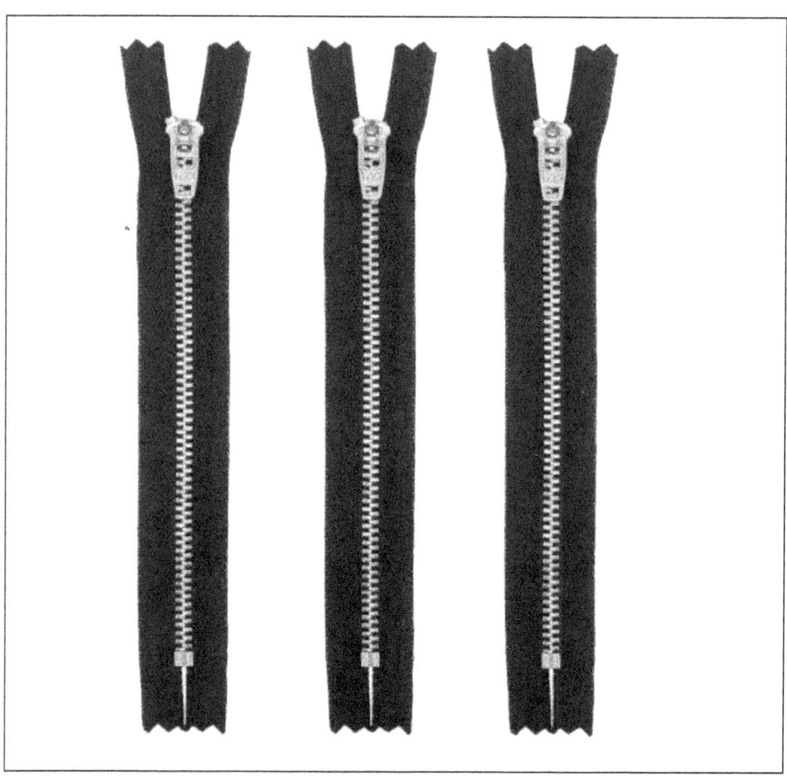

15. Buy Wool, Cotton Cloth or Leather Jackets and Coats

Don't buy outerwear made from petroleum byproducts. Look out for faux down—insist upon real down. Wool provides great warmth. A stylish wool jacket by fiber artist **Arlene Wohl** is shown below. Ruth Bader Ginsburg wore wool clothing made by Ms. Wohl. You can buy one of her pieces of wearable art at www.arlene-wohl.format.com.

Part III
School and Office Supplies

16. Recycle Electronics at Staples or Best Buy

Keep a bag or box for electronic trash, like old cords, radios, batteries, plugs, telephones and other electronic trash and take it to a recycling center when the box is full. Many recycling centers across the country accept electronic trash for recycling.

Best Buy and Staples also accept these products and actually recycle them. There is an abundance of plastic in these products, wire coatings, casings and such. Staples also accepts batteries for recycling.

Staples accepts electronic trash for recycling at all of its 954 stores in the United States. Because of Staples fantastic recycling program, the California Association for Recycling has given Staples its ***Green CARAT Award*** for 2024.

Best Buy also accepts electronic trash at its 1,051 U.S. stores, but does not accept batteries. Best Buy received a ***Green CARAT Award*** in 2022.

17. Don't Buy Plastic Products like Stacking Crates or Trays—Use Metal or Wood

Of course, plastic products are cheap in the short run. But they often crack and don't last. Wood inboxes cost more than plastic trays, but they look better, last longer streams.and don't end up in landfills or in our lakes and Wooden desk drawer tray shown below:

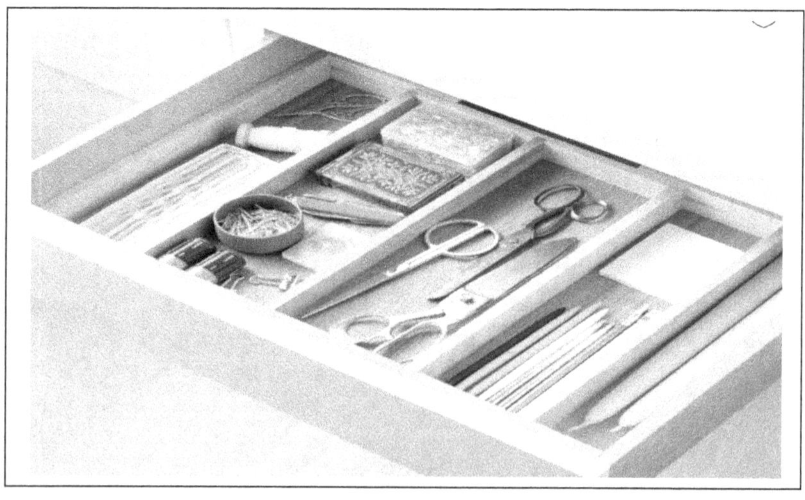

18. Buy Wood or Metal Rulers

Metal rulers and wooden rulers last much longer than plastic ones. I have had a metal ruler that has lasted thirty years and shows no sign of aging. A very sturdy metal rule by **Breman** is shown below:

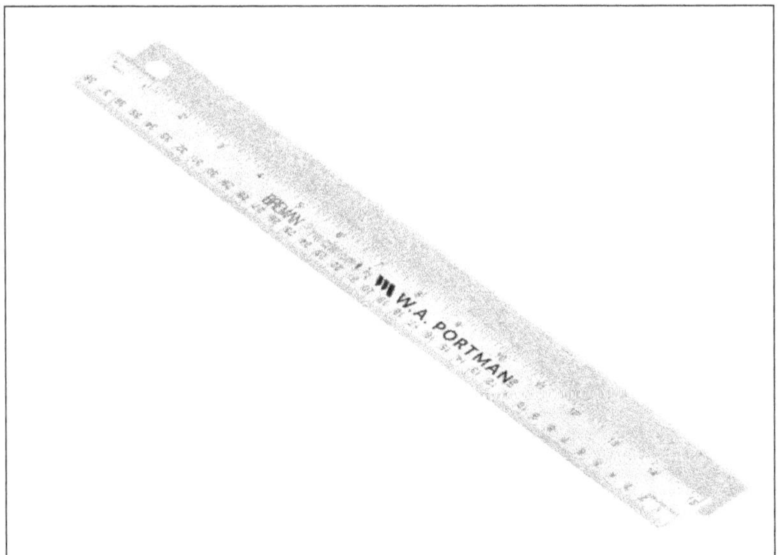

19. Buy Notebooks Made of Cardboard or Metal not Plastic

Cardboard is fully compostable at home as long as it's not coated, you guessed it, with plastic. Many companies are now packaging their products in plain cardboard to cut down on waste. You can also use cardboard boxes to replace plastic storage containers in your home. **Vienrose** 3-ring binder in linen:

20. Metal Pens and Refills

A good metal pen will last a lifetime. Plastic pens become trash and pollute our waterways. A thousand years from now humans, if we still exist, will finds billions of plastic pens in the Earth and floating in gyres of the ocean.

Americans toss 1.6 billion disposable pens annually. These plastic pens end up in landfills and as litter. Some of this plastic waste makes its way to our waterways, where it breaks down into microplastics, polluting our water and harming ocean life.

A classic **Cross** Bailey pen is shown below:

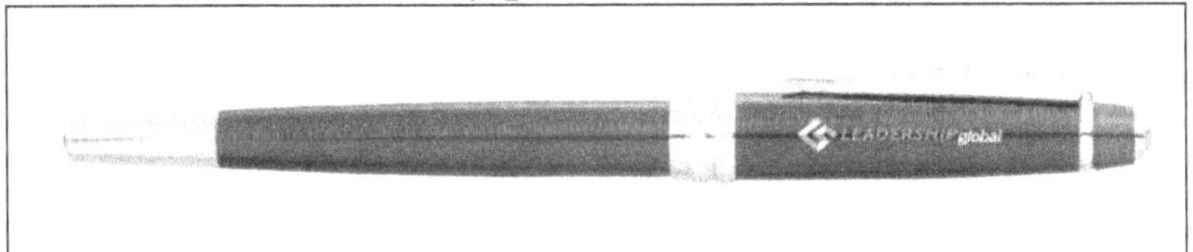

This pen will last a lifetime. Refill cartridges are available at most office supply stores.

21. Buy Metal Paperclips

Plastic paperclips may be colorful, but they break easily. We have been using metal paper clips for more than 100 years.

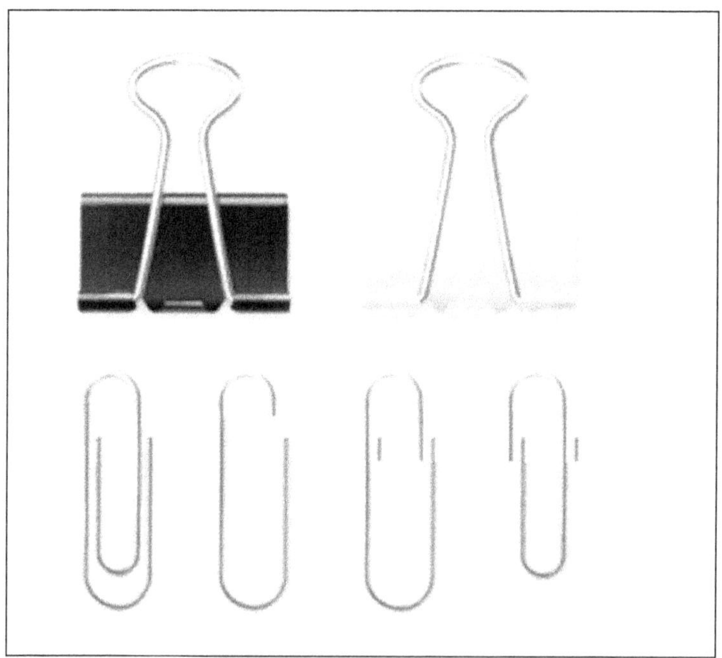

22. Buy Paper Tape Not Plastic Tape

Paper tape works just as well as plastic tape. Paper tape is biodgradable while plastic tape is not. Scotch paper tape, made by **3M**, is pictured below:

23. Buy Paper and Cardboard File Folders

Paper file folders have been used from more than 100 years. Plastic file folders will become trash and will be with us for hundreds of years.

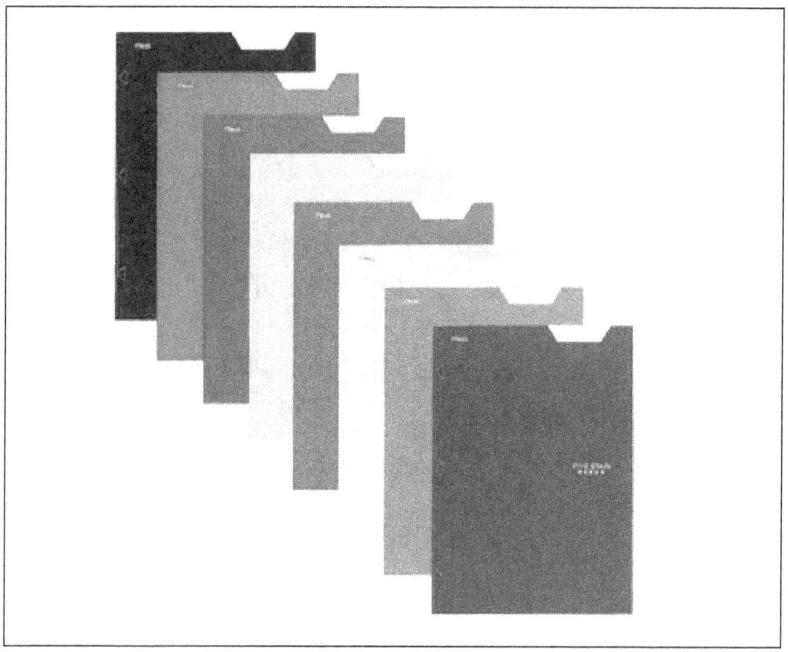

24. Buy Paper Envelopes Not Plastic—Use Fedex and UPS Cardboard Packaging

Fedex and UPS should be banned from using plastic packaging, but until they are you can avoid plastic by using their cardboard boxes and mailing containers.

25. Don't Buy Styrofoam

Styrofoam is a trademarked brand of closedcell extruded polystyrene foam (XPS), commonly called "Blue Board," manufactured as foam building insulation board used in walls, roofs, and foundations as thermal insulation and water barrier. This material is light blue in color and is owned and manufactured by DuPont. DuPont also has produced a line of green and white foam shapes for use in crafts and floral arrangements.

The EPA has reported evidence that styrene is carcinogenic for humans and experimental animals, meaning that there is a positive association between exposure and cancer and that causality is credible.[22]

Polystyrene is slow to degrade, and if disposed of improperly, the foam can leach chemicals into the environment harming water sources. Polystyrene manufacturing is an enormous creator of hazardous waste. Furthermore, polystyrene manufacturing greatly contributes to global warming.

---

[22] (Styrene) Fact Sheet: Support Document (CAS No. 100-42-5) "(PDF). EPA. *December 1994.*

Styrofoam is non-biodegradable and appears to last forever. It's resistant to photolysis, or the breaking down of materials by photons originating from light.

This, combined with the fact that Styrofoam floats, means that large amounts of polystyrene have accumulated along coastlines and waterways around the world. It is a main component of marine debris.

Styrofoam can be recycled, but the market for recycled Styrofoam is diminishing. Many companies no longer will accept polystyrene products. Those that are recycled can be remanufactured into things like cafeteria trays or packaging filler.

Along with the health risks associated with the manufacture of polystyrene, air pollution is another concern. The National Bureau of Standards Center for Fire Research has found 57 chemical byproducts released during the creation of Styrofoam.[23] This not only pollutes the air, but also results in liquid and solid toxic waste that requires proper disposal. Another cause for concern are the brominated flame retardants that are used on Styrofoam products. Research suggests that these chemicals may have negative environmental and health effects. Styrofoam manufacture also uses hydrofluorocarbons (HFCs), which negatively impact the ozone

---

[23] https://rucore.libraries.rutgers.edu/rutgerslib/38329/PDF/1/play/

layer and climate change. HFCs are less detrimental to the ozone than chlorofluorocarbons (CFCs), which were used in the manufacturing of Styrofoam in the past, but it is thought that the impact of HFCs on climate change is much more serious.

Styrofoam is made from petroleum, which is a nonsustainable resource, the production of which creates heavy pollution and accelerates climate change.

Alternatives to Styrofoam

According to the EPA, Americans throw out approximately 25 billion styrofoam cups and take-out containers every year. Compostable food service packaging is very available now. Compostable contain-ers are made using corn starch, palm fiber, peat fiber and wheat stocks; and they're able to break down into soil-enriching compost.

Scientists are developing a suitable replacement for styrofoam. A company named Ecovative Design has created a line of products made from fungi and agricultural waste that are styrofoam-like and aspire to be a more environmentally friendly replacement.[24]

____

[24] www.ecovativedesign.com.

Already, a number of independent restaurants and food service brands worldwide, such as Dunkin' Donuts, have shown how compostable containers can be used as a practical alternative. Several years ago, coffee retailer Tully's began serving its popular beverages in compostable cups.

New York City; Washington, D.C.; Seattle; San Francisco and many more municipalities have announced that food service establishments, stores and manufacturers may not possess, sell, or offer for use single-service Expanded Polystyrene (EPS) foam articles or polystyrene loose fill packaging, such as "packing peanuts."

You, too, can make eco-friendly choices to eliminate the use of Styrofoam. Send a letter to your state representative demanding a statewide ban on polystyrene products.

26. Don't Buy Bubble Wrap

Bubble wrap will remain in landfills and oceans for hundreds, if not thousands, of years. Use cardboard and paper for wrapping delicate items.

Thankfully, there are plenty of safe, eco-sensitive alternatives to Bubble Wrap. **Cushion Lock**, by **3M**, pictured below, and **Hexelwrap,** pictured on the next page, are excellent alternatives. There are other options out there. Corrugated cardboard, paper crinkles, and packaging noodles made from recycled newspaper are all popular choices.

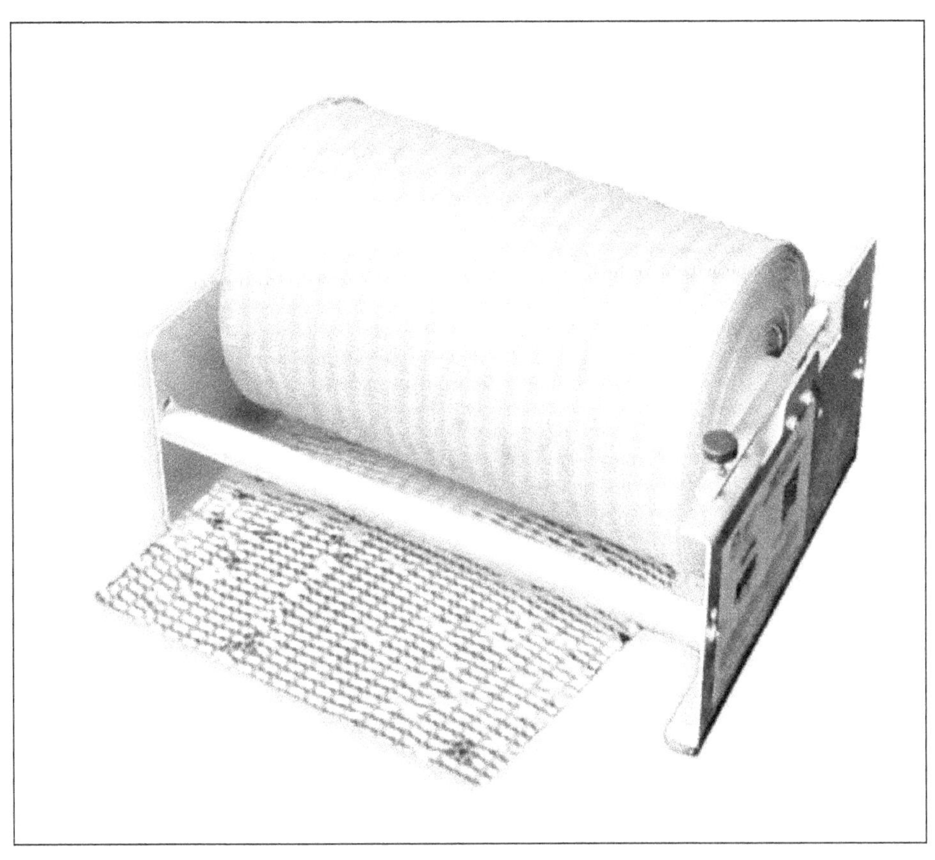

Hexelwrap is made in Canada of 100% (PEFC) Programme for the Endorsement of Forest Certification paper.

27. Don't Buy Plastic Peanuts or Plastic Packing Material

Use cardboard or paper for packing fragile items. Wrap delicate items carefully in tissue paper. Use cardboard between items. Use plenty of heavy-duty brown paper crumpled up to protect breakables. Use the packing materials suggested above, **Cushion Lock** or **Hexelwrap.**

Part IV

In the Kitchen

28. Don't Buy Plastic Kitchen Tools—Buy Wood, Glass or Metal

For example, funnels are made of plastic, metal and glass. Avoid plastic tools. Egg slicers also are made of metal. Knives, spatulas and other tools come with wooden handles as well as plastic. Always choose wood over plastic. Wood is a renewable resource. Look for wood from sustainably-man-aged forests. Wood can replace plastic in household items like cleaning brushes, kitchen utensils and cutting boards. A **Behrens** metal funnel is pictured below:

29. Buy Pottery or Glass Dishes,

Around for millennia, pottery and other fired ceramics offer a stable, waterproof alternative that's good for food storage and tableware. Look for non-toxic glazes. Glass dishes are also attractive, durable and dishwasher safe. **HF Coors** pottery is pictured below.

Available at www.HFCoors.com.

30. Don't Buy Plastic Pitchers or Containers

Glass containers for liquids are far superior to plastic ones. Glass cleans better and does not leach like plastic. You can also use metal tops on glass jars. Glass is dishwasher safe and has been used for thousands of years. A **Libbey** glass pitcher:

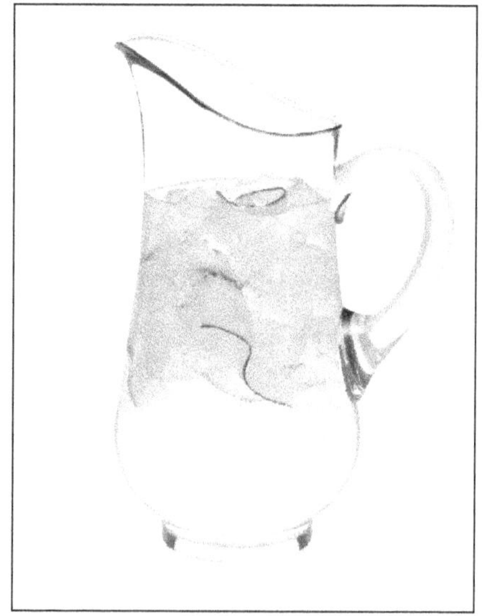

31. Instead of Plastic Wrap, Use Aluminum Foil, Waxed Paper or Glass Jars for Leftovers

Plastic wrap is a waste of resources. It is difficult to recycle small pieces of plastic wrap. Waxed paper is biodegradable. Glass jars are perfect for leftovers.

32. Use Bioplastic Zip Lock Bags

Standard, mass market Zip-lock bags are very handy, but not environmentally friendly. Responsible Products sells compostable zip lock bags.
www.responsibleproducts.shop. Cleanomic also makes bioplastic ziplock bags—
www.cleanomic.com. Myecoworld.com and Amazon.com also sell
compostable ziplock bags. Compostic bags are shown beow:

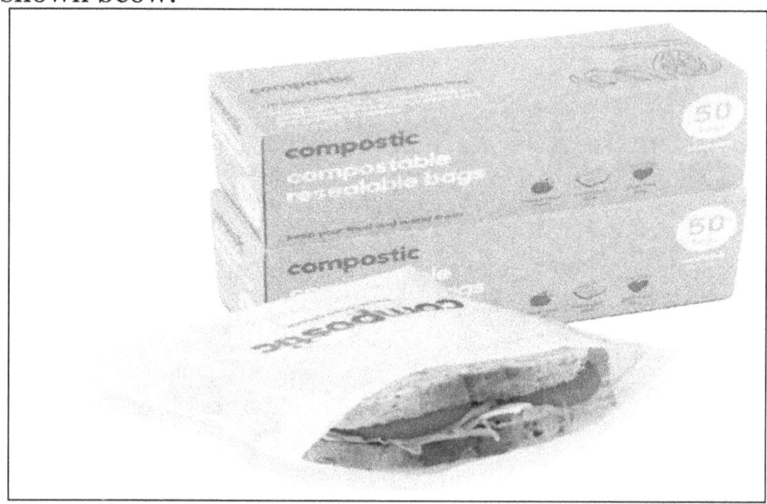

Available at www.composNc.co.

Part V
In the Workshop

33. Buy Metal Tools, Not Plastic Tools

For example, spackling tools are made of plastic or metal. The metal tool will form a better and smoother edge and last much longer. A **Dexter Russell** scraper is pictured below:

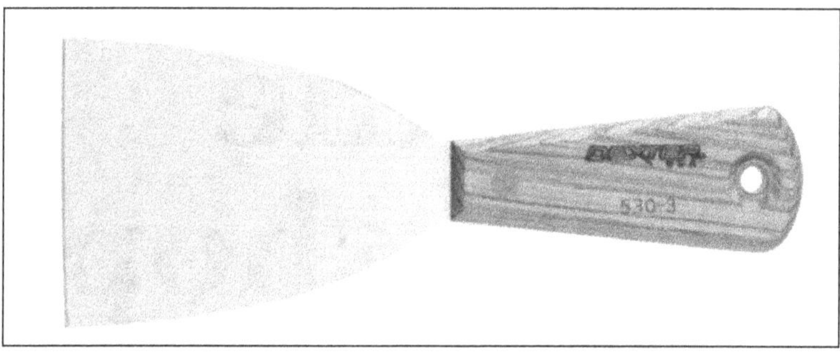

Dexter Russell has been making tools since 1818. Availabe at www.dexter1818.com.

34. Use Copper Pipes Not Plastic Pipes

Copper pipes last longer and will not crack or leak like plastic pipes can. A report from a coalition of U.S. environmental advocacy groups "Journal of Environmental Engineering" has warned of the health risks of PVC plastic and urged public officials against using the material in community drinking water pipes.

PVC is made with vinyl chloride, the same hazardous material released in the fiery train derailment that triggered a public health and environmental crisis in East Palestine, Ohio. It's also a known carcinogen and endocrine disruptor.

Yet, because of its relatively low cost, PVC – polyvinyl chloride – has become a popular option for communities replacing old drinking water pipes and, in particular, the lead pipes and service lines that carry their own public health risks.

The gold standard for years has been copper pipe. Copper pipes are widely regarded as being extremely durable, long-lasting, and reliable. They also require minimal maintenance due to their corrosion resistance, which means that your plumbing will last for years with no additional work required from you. Copper is also very easy to install because it comes in pre-formed pieces that can be connected quickly and easily. Plastic pipes can crack and leak much more easily that properly installed copper piping. Cracked plastic pipe is shown below:

Part VI

In the Garden

35. Use Pottery Pots for Plants Not Plastic

Neither plants nor humans like plastic pots. They are pollution of the future. They will break or crack. A beautiful pottery planter is shown below:

36. Buy Recycled Ocean Trash Products Like Outdoor Rugs

An outdoor rug by Fab Habitat, made from ocean waste, is pictured below:

Available from www.fabhabitat.com.

37. Use Glass or Pottery Vases

Real flowers deserve glass or pottery vases. A pottery vase is shown below:

38. Don't Buy Plastic Plants

Plastic plants aren't eco-friendly. Many fake plants are created in factories using harmful dyes and synthetic materials that aren't easily recycled. And once a fake plant is faded or damaged, it gets thrown in a trash dump where it will probably take hundreds of years to degrade.

39. Use Natural Grass, Not Plastic Grass

While natural grass absorbs carbon dioxide and releases oxygen, artificial turf does the opposite by releasing CO2, methane and a variety of chemicals. Chemical analysis of artificial turf conducted at Yale University found 96 chemicals, 20 percent of them probable carcinogens.

In addition, artificial turf contains highly toxic PFAS or "forever chemicals" linked to lower childhood immunity, endocrine disruption and cancer. Children are especially vulnerable to inhalation, ingestion and dermal absorption, as they are lower to the ground and breathe more quickly.

On top of the chemical makeup of artificial turf, it is also impermeable (unlike natural grass). It requires harsh chemicals for cleaning sweat, mucus, spit, blood, bird droppings, etc., that remain on the surface. And while natural grass has a cooling effect, artificial turf absorbs heat and can become dangerously hot.

Part VII

Furniture

40. Buy Furniture Made with Natural Fibers

Polyvinyl chloride (PVC or vinyl) is the most toxic plastic for our health and the environment. For more than 30 years, leading health, environmental justice, and health-impacted organizations across the country and world have been campaigning to phase out this poison plastic.

During its lifecycle — from production to use to disposal — vinyl releases some of the most toxic chemicals on the planet that have been linked to cancer, birth defects and other serious chronic diseases. PVC production releases dangerous pollutants including vinyl chloride, ethylene dichloride, mercury, dioxins and furans, and PCBs.

Vinyl plastic products expose children and all of us to harmful chemical additives such as phthalates, lead, cadmium and organotins — all substances of very high health concern. Thus, don't buy a vinyl couch. Buy a leather couch or couch made of natural fibers.

41. Use Wood or Metal Picture Frames and Use Glass, Not Plastic in Them

There are many alternatives to plastic frames. If you are framing pictures yourself, **Nielsen** aluminum or wood frames are inexpensive and easy to put together. They are shown below:

Available at www.nielsenbainbridge.com.

42. Don't Buy Plastic Chairs or Plastic Seat Covers

Beautiful fabric seat covers are pictured below.

43. Buy An Organic Mattress

Some mattresses, especially memory foam mattresses or mattresses made of other synthetic materials, are full of petrochemicals, including harmful toxicants. Commonly found chemicals in non-organic mattresses are formaldehyde, benzene, and chemical flame retardants. These chemicals can off-gas, including during your sleep, your mattress can be a significant source of your toxic exposures. 18 million mattresses are disposed of annually in the United States, 200 million worldwide. **Naturepedic** and **Avocado** make excellent organic mattresses. Children are particularly vulnerable to chemicals from nonorganic mattresses. You can also find Naturepedic mattresses in some Crate & Barrel locations, and select Pottery Barn Kids carry Naturepedic beds for children.

Avocado has 15 stores and its mattresses are sold at Living Spaces. A **Naturepedic** mattress is pictured below:

Available at www.naturepedic.com

Part VIII

Accessories

44. Buy Wood Clothes Pins and Hangers

Wooden clothes by **Kevin's Quality Close Pins** are shown below:

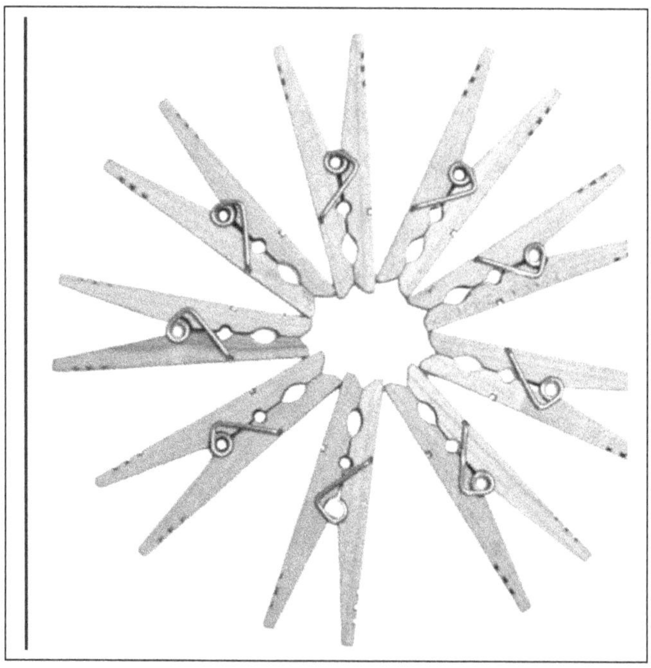

Available at www.ladyandthecarpenter.com.

45. Buy Metal or Wood Eyeglasses, not Plastic

American Optical, Art Craft and **Randolph** make metal frames in the United States. **American Optical** and **Randolph** frames are used by the Air Force. **Randolph's** aviator frames are pictured below:

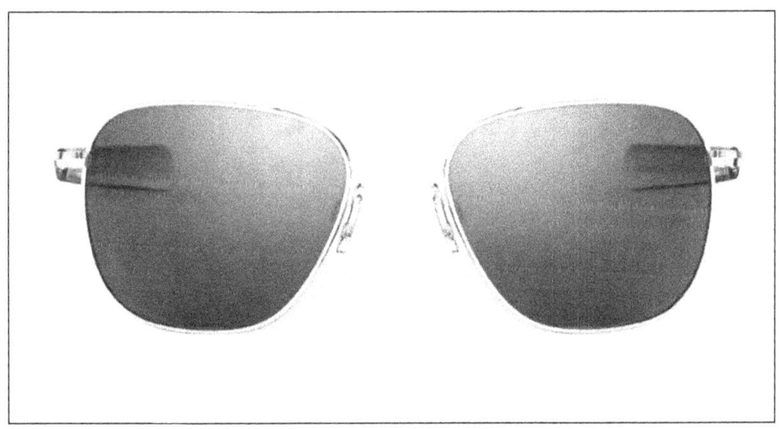

Available at www.randolphusa.com.

Part IX
Toys

46. Buy Wooden or Metal Childrens Toys

Plastic toys break easily. Wooden and metal toys last for many years and can be handed down from child to child and to grandchildren. **Maple Landmark's** wooden train is shown below as is **Crocodile Creek's** wooden puzzle. In addition, plastic toys are usually made in Asia and therefore have a large carbon footprint. Available at www.maplelandmark.com and www.crockodilecreek.com.

47. Don't Buy Balloons

Balloons are often seen as fun, harmless decorations. But they become deadly litter as soon as they are released into the air and forgotten.

Deliberate releases of tens, hundreds or sometimes thousands of balloons are common sights at weddings, graduations, memorials, sporting events and other celebrations. These fleeting feel-good acts inflict long-lasting and potentially deadly consequences on the environment and wildlife. Balloons filled with helium – a finite and rapidly dwindling resource – travel hundreds or even thousands of miles. They land as litter on beaches, rivers, lakes, oceans, forests and other natural areas.

The two most common types of balloons are Mylar and latex. Mylar balloons, also called foil balloons, are made from plastic nylon sheets with a metallic coating and will never biodegrade. They also cause thousands of power outages every year when they come into contact with power lines or circuit breakers.

While some manufacturers claim that natural latex balloons made from liquid rubber are biodegradable, they still take years to break down because they are mixed with plasticizers and other chemical additives that hinder the biodegradation process. Other latex balloons are synthetic, made from a petroleum derivative called neoprene and will remain in the environment indefinitely, breaking down into smaller and smaller pieces over time.

Both Mylar and latex balloons are a significant threat to wildlife, livestock and pets, which can be injured or killed from eating balloon fragments, getting tangled in long balloon ribbons or strings, or being spooked by the falling debris.

Part X

Taking Action

48. Participate in Beach Cleanups

There are beach cleanups of plastic trash all over the country. You can find them by Googling "beach cleanup" and the name of your city. The following links are to beach cleanups around the nation:

Alabama-
https://www.alpals.org/index.cfm/programs/coastalclean-
up/#:~:text=The%20third%20Saturday%20in%20September,Coastal%20Cleanup%20time%20in%20Alabama!

Alaska-https://marinedebris.noaa.gov/alaska

California-https://www.parks.ca.gov/?page_id=27144
Connecticut-https://www.savethesound.org/whatwe-do/healthy-waters/cleanups-and-marine-debris/

Delaware-
https://dnrec.alpha.delaware.gov/coastalcleanup/

Florida-https://floridadep.gov/rcp/coral/content/shorebased-beach-cleanups

Georgia-https://www.unitedwayvolunteers.org/agency/detail/?agency_id=12907

Hawaii--https://808cleanups.org

Louisianahttps://scienceforourcoast.org/beachsweep/

Maine-https://www.cascobay.org/how-to-help/coastalcleanups/

Maryland-https://www.ccamd.org/chesapeakecleanup-project/
Massacusetts--https://www.mass.gov/coastsweep

Mississippihttp://coastalcleanup.extension.msstate.edu

New Hampshire-

https://www.blueoceansociety.org/beachcleanup/newhampshire-coastal-cleanup/

New Jersey-https://www.njclean.org/ourprograms/adopt-a-beach/overview

New York-http://www.nysbeachcleanup.org/#:~:text=during%20the%202022%20New%20York%20State%20Beach%2

North Carolinahttps://www.nccoast.org/project/coastal-cleanups/

Oregon-https://www.seasideor.com/beachcoins/#:~:text=Join%20A%20Group%20Cleanup%3A&text=Consider%20also%20joining%20the%20thousands,in%202020%20despite%20the%20pandemic.

Rhode Islandhttp://www.crmc.ri.gov/news/2021_0915_cleanup.html

South Carolina-https://www.dnr.sc.gov/bsrs/

Texas-https://texasadoptabeach.org/volunteer/cleanups/index.html

Virginia-
https://parks.virginiabeach.gov/eventsinformation/speci
al-events/international-coastalcleanup

Washingtonhttps://www.unitedwayvolunteers.org/ag

ency/detail/?agency_id=12907

49. Recycle All Plastic

Only ten states require deposits on plastic, glass and metal bottles and cans. The ten states are California, Connecticut, Hawaii, Iowa, Maine, Massachusetts, Michigan, New York, Oregon and Vermont. So. if you live in one of these states, make sure that you return them for recycling. In other states you can put bottles and cans into recycling bins.

Electronic Trash

Electronic trash, including computers, plastic-coated wiring, batteries and appliances can be recycled. **Staples** accepts electronic trash for recycling at all of its 954 stores in the United States. Because of Staples fantastic recycling program, the California Association for Recycling has given Staples its *Green CARAT Award* for 2024.

Best Buy also accepts electronic trash at its 1,051 U.S. stores, but does not accept batteries. Best Buy received a *Green CARAT Award* in 2022.

50. Donate to the California Association for Recycling All Trash (CARAT)

CARAT publishes this book as well as Plastic Pollution Solution and The Age of Plastic, a children's book. CARAT is a non-profit 501(c)(3) organization. Donations to CARAT are tax-deductible. CARAT is dedicated to reducing plastic pollution worldwide. CARAT's website is www.calrecycles.com:

Other Books on plastic pollution:

Available from bookstores or   www.inprintbooks.us.

The Age of
Plastic

by George Poppel

Available from bookstores or www.inprintbooks.us